PRO SPORTS: SHOULD GOVERNMENT INTERVENE?

John Charles Daly, *Moderator*

Jack Kemp
Lee MacPhail
Ed Garvey
Roger Noll

A Round Table held on February 22, 1977
and sponsored by
the American Enterprise Institute for Public Policy Research
Washington, D.C.

This pamphlet contains the edited transcript of
one of a series of AEI forums.
These forums offer a medium for
informal exchanges of ideas on current policy problems
of national and international import.
As part of AEI's program of providing opportunities
for the presentation of competing views,
they serve to enhance the prospect
that decisions within our democracy will be based
on a more informed public opinion.
AEI forums are also available on
audio and color-video cassettes.

AEI Forum 4

© 1977 by American Enterprise Institute
for Public Policy Research, Washington, D.C.
Permission to quote from
or reproduce materials in this publication is granted
when due acknowledgment is made.

ISBN 0-8447-2097-6
Library of Congress Catalog Card No. 77-078705

Printed in United States of America

JOHN CHARLES DALY, former ABC News chief and moderator of the Round Table: This public policy forum, part of a series presented by the American Enterprise Institute, addresses the question whether the government should intervene in professional sports. The fact is, of course, the government has intervened for a long time.

Two of our three coequal branches of government, the judicial and the legislative, have affected the character of professional sports substantially. Mr. Justice Oliver Wendell Holmes ruled in *Federal Baseball* v. *National League,* back in 1922, that the business of giving exhibitions of baseball was not within interstate commerce for the purposes of the federal antitrust laws. Behind this bulwark, baseball waged continuous battle for years to sustain its reserve clause, which defines the character and the restrictions of service for professional baseball players.

Only last year, in 1976, under terms of a contract between owners and the players association, new rules opened a free-agent status to a player after five or six years service in the majors.

In football, a former Washington Redskin, James McCoy "Yazoo" Smith, filed an antitrust suit charging that the college draft constituted a per se violation under antitrust law, and an earlier recent case, *Mackey* v. *National Football League,* involved an antitrust challenge to the

1

NFL's so-called Rozelle Rule, which established criteria under which a veteran football player might become a free agent. Both Yazoo Smith and Mackey triumphed, and, in the closing weeks of 1976, *Mackey* was sustained on appeal by the Eighth Circuit Court. The Supreme Court's response to repeated attempts to overturn Mr. Justice Holmes on baseball's reserve clause and antitrust immunity was that the Congress had noted this matter and the Congress should legislate any change. In the case of football, the Eighth Circuit Court of Appeals, sustaining the antitrust violation in *Mackey* v. *National Football League,* concluded with a primer on how football could, in arm's length collective bargaining between management and players, earn what is known as the "labor exemption" to antitrust liability.

As of this moment, it can be said that the management and the players associations in baseball and basketball have, in broad terms, essentially made their peace. And in early 1977, an agreement in principle was effected by management and players in football.

A House Select Committee on Professional Sports in 1976 energetically investigated "the apparent instability prevailing in the sports industries for major professional team sports"—baseball, basketball, football, and hockey. The committee recommended that a successor oversight committee be ,tablished to conduct inquiries into the need for legislation with respect to all professional sports.

That's it in a nutshell. Our question is, Pro sports: should the government intervene? And I will add, "further." We are dealing tonight with professional team sports and, as the composition of our panel indicates, concentrating on football and baseball.

Congressman Kemp was an all-AFL quarterback, the AFL player of the year in 1965, a cofounder and former president of the AFL players association, and a former member of the NFL Players Association Executive Committee and Players Pension Board, and he is now in his seventh year in the House of Representatives. Congressman Kemp, do you think a further House inquiry into legislation with respect to professional sports is wise or necessary?

JACK KEMP, United States representative (Republican, New York) : I generally favor having the Congress consider legislation that would make all professional sports equal under the antitrust laws. No sport should receive separate treatment. The same antitrust laws should apply to all sports, with certain partial exemptions to provide competitive strength, to make the game attractive to the consumer, and to protect the rights of individual players.

That should be the direction of any congressional inquiry, but one is likely to go far beyond that because there are members of Congress who have a propensity for going far beyond rather limited mandates. There are those who would abolish the option clause, there are those who would abolish the draft, and there are those who would probably go even beyond that.

A further House inquiry will be helpful because it will give all sides a chance to make their point. Other than that, I would favor a hands-off approach by government, relying instead upon the self-regulating mechanisms of the business, with the strong collective bargaining environment that has been built up in sports in the last ten years or fifteen years.

MR. DALY: Mr. Garvey, as general counsel of the National Football League Players Association and, since 1971, its executive director, I believe, you have been in the front line in the conflicts between management and players in recent years. Do you see a future of self-regulation or of government intervention?

ED GARVEY, executive director, National Football League Players Association: Government first intervened by giving tremendous powers to the owners by exempting them from the antitrust laws when they pooled their television rights. Congress intervened again when it allowed the merger of the American Football League and the National Football League without requiring any protection for the fans or the players.

Government has intervened in a way that has made it very difficult for self-regulation. The player unions are relatively weak, but the owner organizations are very strong and can split expenses and work their will pretty much as they want to.

Government has intervened on only one side, to build up the power of management. Self-regulation will require stronger efforts by the players, possibly to achieve joint selection of league commissioners to allow for evenhanded regulation.

MR. DALY: Mr. MacPhail, your thirty-four years in baseball as business manager, general manager, team executive, and league president have given you a very broad perspective. What do you think of the present situation in baseball vis-à-vis the government?

LEE MACPHAIL, President, American League: We have had problems in baseball, just as the other sports have had. I think we have made progress in solving those problems. We have reached an agreement with our players association that is fine and fair for the players and the owners. The need for the reserve system was recognized by both sides, and together we constructed a reserve system that both sides can live with.

In regard to government supervision of professional sports, our country is based on a laissez-faire system, with government supervision and regulation only where they have been shown to be necessary. It may not be a perfect system for everybody—there is a slip here and there—but professional sports have been conducted responsibly. Although we welcome the present congressional investigation, · cooperate with it to the fullest, and expect the results to be helpful and not a hindrance to professional sports, we basically believe that there should be no government regulation.

MR. DALY: Professor Noll, your book *Government and the Sports Business,* which you edited as a senior fellow at the Brookings Institution, is an exhaustive examination of the economics of organized sports. Will a future be worked out within the sports industry that is economically sound?

ROGER NOLL, visiting professor, Graduate School of Business, Stanford University: Yes, the economics of professional sports look good but not quite as good as in the past. Obviously, the golden days of being an owner are long since gone.

Two of the five special arrangements enjoyed by professional sports have gone, or are going, by the wayside. One is the control of the player market by allocating players among teams, giving teams monopoly rights to bargain with the pool of players assigned to it. The stronger player unions have pretty much undone that, both through the courts and through collective bargaining. Obviously, the players will claim an increasing share of the revenue of professional sports, as the unions gain strength.

Changes in the tax laws are rapidly eroding the use of professional sports as a tax shelter. Congress enacted a law that cut this tax shelter substantially. Currently, the Internal Revenue Service is fighting in the courts to reduce the tax-shelter aspect of professional sports even more.

5

But three special arrangements will continue to make professional sports a more profitable enterprise for both owners and players than a competitive business would be. First is the arrangement with regard to stadiums. In most sports, stadiums now are more numerous than the number of teams. Cities have to engage in competitive bidding and make incredibly foolish rental offers to persuade a team to stay in the city or to move from another city. Recently, we saw such an activity between stadium authorities in New Jersey and those in New York City concerning where the New York Jets would play. And just before that, we saw bidding between San Diego and Washington, D.C., for a baseball team.

Second, in broadcasting, as Mr. Garvey mentioned, the leagues can bargain as a legal monopoly—rather than as a consortium of teams, as several consortia, or even as individual teams—to sell broadcasting rights to ball games in all sports. This practice substantially increases the revenue for all teams at the expense, of course, of the networks. I don't feel terribly sorry for the networks, but, as a result of this practice, the fans have access to less sports broadcasting.

Third, we still have territorial rights, perhaps the most egregious wrong of all monopolistic practices in professional sports. The nation's capital can subsist without a baseball team for six or seven years. The number of franchises can be controlled by owners, who can dole them out just as any other monopolist would, creating a contrived scarcity. Many more cities could support teams if the supply were not limited. In recent years, as sports have become more popular, the response of the monopolist has been predictable—ticket prices go up and up and up. In a competitive industry, higher ticket prices induce new firms to compete, but the monopolist simply takes in higher revenues. Now the owners share in the take with the players and the union. The financing looks good, but the fan is being ripped off.

Mr. MacPhail: I don't think the fan is being ripped off. The average price of all the tickets sold in the American League last year was $3.08. No other entertainment is as reasonably priced as that. A fan can still sit in the bleachers for $1. Professional baseball clubs have not been making money by gouging the public. I don't think the record shows that the owners have made unfair and unconscionable profits in any sport.

Congressman Kemp: For thirteen years I was a part of that so-called monopoly. The American Football League, from which I came to Congress, started as a competitive business to the National Football League. I would remind Professor Noll, who takes a very academic but rather unrealistic view of professional sports in America today, of conditions in 1957. Mr. Garvey could probably tell us the average professional football salary today but in 1957, when I started with the Detroit Lions, Bobby Layne was quarterback of that team at a salary of about $19,000 or $20,000. He was the premier quarterback in professional football. Salaries have increased substantially. There were only thirty-two men on a team and only twelve teams in the National Football League when the American Football League started.

In the relatively short period since then, the number of teams has increased to twenty-eight. There are now player limits of forty or forty-two, with five or ten more on taxi squads. Professional sports are shown more on television, and more people are watching sports. More people—and especially more young people—have access to the healthy influence of competitive athletics on television than ever before.

By any reasonable standard, these are the things that the fans want—a good game, accessible on television, with tickets at a price they can afford (ticket prices are subject to much more than the so-called monopolistic practices that Professor Noll talks about). Generally, the people of America are seeing more sports than ever before. Athletes are now earning more in professional sports, which are open to far more young men. Someday there will also be more professional sports for women, like tennis. On the record, professional sports have done much better than Professor Noll says.

MR. GARVEY: Congressman Kemp focuses on the athlete, pointing out that the athlete was earning only $19,000 then, but earns $40,000 now. Congress tends to do the same thing—when it considers regulations, it takes a look at the player.

The simple fact is, we have never known how much the owners make. We have never been able to look into the records of the owners in professional baseball or football to see what that profit picture really is. And the test is not what Bobby Layne was making back in 1957, compared with what he would make today. The test is whether he was getting a proper share of the revenues then, and whether the athlete today is getting a proper share.

Whenever people talk about regulation, they talk about regulating the athlete but not the owner. If the government is going to move into professional sports, it should look at how much money is being made, whether stadium rental is fair to the taxpayer, whether a team should be allowed to move just by announcing that it has been losing money, and things of that nature. There is no need to worry that players today are making more than Bobby Layne made in 1957.

8

PROFESSOR NOLL: Congressman Kemp, unknowingly maybe, gave an excellent speech in favor of competitive free enterprise. He talked about how the American Football League changed things. It surely did. Considering its effects on NFL expansion, it more than doubled the number of jobs available to professional football players. It substantially increased the availability of football to people who want to attend a game in person and to people who want to watch one on television. In fact, the number of televised football games expanded fourfold as a consequence of this competition between the two leagues. As a result of this competition, the leagues fought to get into Atlanta and other cities. They fought to hire players, and players' salaries went up.

The AFL gave Congressman Kemp the opportunity to prove that he is an all-star quarterback. He never had the opportunity to play professional football until football was a competitive business, and look how good he was. That is exactly what happens when there is competition. There is more for the fans, more for the players, a more exciting enterprise. The merger put an end to that competition.

In professional baseball, which has never had that competition, we still find the strange mystical dance in which the politicians, the owners, and the players engage when they debate about a baseball team for Washington, D.C., or about who will play in which stadium and why. Will the football Giants and the Yankees desert Yankee Stadium in mid-construction and leave New York with an $80 million bill?

The dance of the revolving franchise happens because franchises are too scarce. There are potential owners who would like to have a baseball team and who have enough money to operate one—the $12 million or so necessary to get into the sport. There are fans in Washington, D.C., and other places who would like to prove that their cities can support the game, but they have no opportunity to do so.

The number of franchises is decided on the basis of the financial interests of the existing owners and nothing else.

The next big public policy issue in sports will be whether we can protect the integrity of the sport and protect owners from having some teams fold in mid-season because of financial difficulties, while still allowing the number of teams to be governed by the interests of the fans. I would like to see that happen in all the sports, but nobody seems to be lobbying very hard for it. The Amalgamated Fans of America has yet to be formed to bargain collectively or to lobby Congress for relief from this particular monopolistic practice.

MR. MACPHAIL: It is irresponsible to say, as Professor Noll just did, that the Yankees threatened to leave Yankee Stadium in the middle of the construction of an $80 million stadium. I have paid close attention to that situation, and I was never aware of any such threats by the Yankees.

PROFESSOR NOLL: The press may have been misleading about this, but my understanding was that both the Giants and the Yankees at one time threatened to leave Yankee Stadium after the city purchased it from the Yankees and before renovation was complete. The Giants, of course, did move to Jersey Meadows.

MR. MACPHAIL: Mr. Garvey also said that our replies only addressed what was happening to the athletes. My reply concentrated upon the price of tickets and the profits of ownership. I would like to hear him or Professor Noll say whether either of those was out of line.

MR. GARVEY: Profits are not necessarily excessive in baseball or football or hockey. We do not know whether they are or not. Congress probably does not know because every time it has tried to get that information, the owners have said that this is a free enterprise system, and so they don't have to divulge it. When the American Basketball Association and the National Basketball Association wanted to merge, Senator Ervin asked the owners to bring their books and records, including their personal income tax statements, to show whether they were really losing money, and the owners said, "no," that was not what they had in mind.

If it is announced that an athlete is making $100,000, the fans say he is over-priced and pampered. But they do not know whether the owners of the Washington Redskins are making a half-million dollars or, as they say, losing a half-million dollars. They do not know what the average profit is for pro teams, and, therefore, they do not know whether the fan is getting a fair shake. That was my point.

CONGRESSMAN KEMP: There would not have been any argument about profit in pro sports a number of years ago—especially in pro football—because it was not a very profitable business, if indeed it made a profit at all. The game did not have television exposure, and it did not attract the fans to the extent that it does today. I compared my 1957 experience with 1977 in order to show how far professional sports, especially football, have come. And, as Professor Noll is aware, I do favor competitive free enterprise. That is why I support these pro sports.

Professor Noll says that he cannot buy a professional baseball franchise. Nor can I. I cannot buy a McDonald's franchise, though I would love to have one. But still some entrepreneur can start a new enterprise, if there is a market for his product or league, just as the World Football League, the American Football League, and the Canadian Football League did.

The monopoly in sports is a natural monopoly, which is quite different from a government-instituted or government-promoted monopoly. The fact is, the American Football

11

League and the World Football League did get started. Professional sports should be treated not necessarily like an ordinary business but more like a franchise operation. When the Buffalo Bills play the New York Jets, they are not out to wipe each other off the economic field or to wipe each other out financially. They are out to beat each other in that football game. That is not economic competition. The two teams share the television and radio revenues, they share the gate, and they share the talent so that they can be as competitive as possible on the football field. This is the only way that smaller cities with smaller markets—such as Buffalo and Green Bay—can possibly compete with New York, Los Angeles, and other large cities.

When we were very young and played baseball or football or any other sport on the street, the two captains chose players in a reciprocal fashion so that we would have a good game, predicated upon relatively equal talent on each team. That method enhances the competition all of us want, and it ultimately enhances the salary and rewards of the players and the owners by appealing to consumers, that is, the fans. "If it ain't broke, don't fix it."

MR. DALY: It would be useful if one of you described the present situation with regard to reserve clauses and similar contract clauses in baseball and football. Would you discuss baseball, Mr. MacPhail?

MR. MACPHAIL: In baseball, each contract once had a reserve clause binding the player to play each succeeding year. That was struck down through a grievance procedure brought by the players association in the case of Andy Messersmith. In effect, it wiped out the reserve system as we had known it in baseball. The players association and the player relations committee of the owners then entered into collective bargaining to set up a new reserve system. The players association readily saw the need for a reserve system.

Congress and the courts have also recognized that need, particularly in baseball, where we have a problem of developing players and bringing young players along in a minor league structure.

To answer the question, we have negotiated a new reserve system, which, in return for the money the club has spent on player development, entitles it to six years of that player's service. At the end of that time, the player can elect to be a free agent, if he so desires. At the end of five years, he can ask that his contract be traded, and if that is done, he can veto a certain number of teams that may want him. For the player who becomes a free agent, we have a rather complicated reentry system designed to maintain competitive balance and, as Congressman Kemp pointed out, to protect the smaller franchises and enable them to compete against the stronger ones.

MR. DALY: Is this a reentry draft?

MR. MACPHAIL: That is correct. Half of the teams can draft free agents, but the teams are limited in the number of players that they may sign.

MR. DALY: And the team's standing order in the draft is in reverse order from its standing in the previous seasons played. What about football?

MR. GARVEY: Since 1963, pro football has had the Rozelle Rule, which sets the compensation for a player who has played out his contract. In the old days, we had the "option clause," and we hope those old days are gone forever. When a player tried to sign with another team, that team had to compensate his former team with a player of like quality. If they could not agree, then the commissioner would name compensation for that player. The court in the *Mackey* case ruled that there was virtually no difference between that

13

and the baseball reserve clause, because the team wishing to sign the player would not sign him out of fear of this unknown compensation they would have to pay. Basically, there was little difference. Both sports used "competitive balance" to justify their reserve system.

Sports announcers say that on any given Sunday in professional football any team might beat any other. That does not exactly represent the facts or my idea of competitive balance. Nor does the fact that New Orleans has never won half of its games in a season exactly represent competitive balance. The reserve system did not bring about competitive balance. In fact, it has locked certain teams into a winning situation, and certain other teams into a losing situation, and changing that is a very slow process. In essence, there was no difference in the reserve systems of professional football, baseball, basketball, and hockey. Now all four are moving toward a different system, in large measure because the courts have said there has to be an element of fairness. The owners cannot say they need control of players in order to bring about balance when they do not control coaches or general managers—or even the profit-sharing or the gate-sharing in some sports. They just want control of the players. The interference by the courts in this situation has been very helpful in changing the system in all sports.

CONGRESSMAN KEMP: I would agree that there has to be fairness. My point at the beginning of the program was that the process can be carried out better through the self-governing mechanism of collective bargaining than by Congress or politicians, who hold what I consider to be a rather unrealistic view of the problems that Mr. Garvey has so eloquently stated. I have no quarrel with his statement. The system ought to be fair—to the players, to the owners, to the sport, and to the fans.

14

To reiterate, I happen to believe that if Congress had tried to interject itself when Mr. Garvey was negotiating with the owners, the agreements would not have been worked out. Some in Congress would have made a public utility out of pro sports, and that would not serve the interests of the fans, the players, or the owners, certainly not the taxpayers.

PROFESSOR NOLL: A central issue in the debate about the extent to which restrictive practices are necessary in sports centers on the issue of competitive balance. We have heard it mentioned several times here, and we should have it made clear on the record. In any systematic analysis of the competitive balance of leagues—as measured by the mixing phenomenon in league standings, by the dispersion in won/lost record between the best and the worst teams, or by almost any other kind of statistical measure of balance—there is absolutely no evidence that competitive balance is accomplished by the mechanism for dealing with players.

In basketball, for example, when there was one basketball league with a restrictive player system, basketball players were not paid very much, and the Boston Celtics won every year. When the American Basketball Association came into existence, and competition for players and for cities came into existence along with it, that dynasty suddenly disappeared. I would not pretend to argue that competition caused the demise of the Celtics. Lots of other things happened. The fact remains, however, there is no evidence that a restrictive player market helps the fans in terms of competitive balance.

I once went through a list of the teams that had made the play-offs in professional football in the last seven years, and the same teams appeared year after year after year. Ed Garvey mentioned New Orleans as a perennial loser, but there are about ten teams in professional football that have not made a play-off in ten years. If it is true that the restrictive system in the player market causes competitive balance, it is, indeed, a slow-working process. One wonders if all the restrictions on a player's right to live where he wants are justified by a mixing phenomenon that takes more than a decade to work.

CONGRESSMAN KEMP: In practice it does not take a decade. Many teams have worked their way up in the league standings through use of the draft. The draft is not the only way a team can move up in the standings—there are many tangible and intangible aspects of professional sports competition—talent, coaching, fan support, ownership.

Before the draft, two or three teams dominated professional football. Since the draft was instituted by Bert Bell, around 1940, there is evidence that it has brought about a more competitive climate.

Some of the statements made here deal in the abstract. I am not referring to the remarks by Ed Garvey, who is there at the front lines, doing an able job of representing the interests, as he sees them, of the players. But take Professor Noll's remarks about, for instance, television. On the one hand, he is very much interested in bringing more televised games to the fans. On the other hand, he opposes the pooling of the television rights of professional football, for example, which not only gave professional football greater access to television but also gave the fans the opportunity to see "away" games. Until pooling was allowed, there were no telecasts of the home team's out-of-town games. There is more television coming back into those NFL franchise cities now because of pooling. And, if it had not been for pooling, there would not have been a successful American Football League. Pooling was an important ingredient in making the game popular. It has exposed the game to ever more fans throughout the United States.

16

PROFESSOR NOLL: Congressman, the year before the Sports Broadcasting Act was passed, there were three separate organizations of National Football League teams—three separate consortia—and each had nationwide television games on Sundays. In addition to these three competitive NFL broadcasts, there was the AFL broadcast—making a total of four.

CONGRESSMAN KEMP: And they were on two networks—on only two networks.

PROFESSOR NOLL: No, they were on four—all three of the major networks, plus a fourth network of independents.

CONGRESSMAN KEMP: When the American Football League started, it sued the National Football League for operating on two networks.

PROFESSOR NOLL: Right.

CONGRESSMAN KEMP: And then, when the National Football League changed from two networks to only one by pooling its TV rights, it was sued by the antitrust division of the Justice Department. So, the NFL was on opposite sides of antitrust litigation within two years.

MR. GARVEY: But the problem for the World Football League was that the Justice Department did nothing when the National Football League had the ABC, NBC, and CBS networks tied up, because of their pooling arrangements. In order to tie up all three networks, the NFL probably was willing to take in less total television revenue than it could have obtained, and so the World Football League could not break into the television market. Because Congress allowed that sort of pooling, and because the Justice Department did not act, the World Football League could not survive as a viable entity. When such decisions are contemplated by the government, it has a responsibility to look at the consequences. That decision not to act helped bring about the demise of the World Football League, along with some bad management in the WFL.

MR. MACPHAIL: It's hard to believe anyone would think there isn't enough professional football on television today. [Laughter.]

MR. GARVEY: There's too much baseball.

MR. DALY: Let's go back to the fan. Coming back to what Professor Noll said, I cried along with many other Washingtonians when the Senators moved away. But, I can also remember days when the Senators were lucky if a hundred people came to Griffith Stadium to watch them play baseball. That is not fan support. The people of Washington have no inherent right to a baseball team, when the record shows such a lack of support.

The other side of my question is about the fan himself. I am happy that collective bargaining, at arm's length, has improved the players' income prospects, pensions, and all that sort of thing. And I am saddened that football has felt the sting and the lash of inflation, as we all have. But, such factors have brought about the day when football ticket prices are very high. Because the economics are so demanding, can we let this become a spectator sport for only an elite group? Who wants to start?

MR. MACPHAIL: I will start. I know Professor Noll won't agree with what I have to say because I know he has a different view on this subject, but I honestly believe that any city that has a proper market area, that can support baseball, that has a proper facility, that has potential owners, that has the necessary capital, that has the confidence of the locale—any city that is in that situation in time will get a major league baseball club. The same is probably true of the other sports.

We have had a problem in Washington that we are trying to work out, but Washington did not meet all those qualifications at the time it lost its club. The Senators would not have been allowed to move if there had been owners willing to take on the Washington club and run the risk of operating it in professional baseball.

PROFESSOR NOLL: I do not disagree with Mr. MacPhail as much as he might think. I suspect that in time, if a new owner is willing to lay out $12 million or $15 million, Washington can have a baseball team. Admittedly, media coverage of professional sports occurs in a circus atmosphere, and potential owners say things to the press that perhaps are not backed up by their bank accounts. But when Bob Short moved the Senators to Texas, there were at least three groups which said they would pay on the order of $10 million to $12 million for the team. And, subsequently, several other groups have emerged to try to get a team. Part of the problem is that the negotiations have to be worked out to the satisfaction of the owners of the existing teams.

Mr. Daly said that only a hundred people might show up for a game. Well, I used to be among those few, and I enjoyed the solitude of the stands. [Laughter.]

MR. DALY: How about extrapolating the cost of the game among those hundred spectators. Would you have paid the admission price then?

PROFESSOR NOLL: Obviously not, but if there are people who are willing to give a team a try, why should we feel that the firms in any industry should be guaranteed against failure? If some people believe that they can sell baseball in Washington, D.C.—and Bill Veeck once said it was a baseball gold mine for the right owner—then let them try, as long as that exercise in trying can be prevented from causing damage to the sport itself.

Mr. MacPhail raised the issue of ticket prices, and he is absolutely right, incidentally, that the American League deserves plaudits for being atypical in keeping ticket prices low. In general, the spread of ticket prices in baseball between the most expensive and the least expensive teams is quite narrow, compared with most sports. There is a factor of only about two between the teams with the cheapest and most expensive ticket prices.

In professional basketball, a single sold-out game in Madison Square Garden brings in almost as much revenue for the Knickerbockers as some other teams get in an entire season. There is an enormous spread in ticket prices in most of the other sports as well, and there is much of what economists call excess demand. For example, there are long waiting lists for season tickets at existing prices for Washington Redskins games. Prices are very high, yes, but many people are willing to pay them. In fact, so many are willing to pay them that in the very best markets there is room for another team.

MR. GARVEY: As usual, I'd like to defend NFL management. [Laughter.]

One of the difficult problems for football is its very short season, which makes comparisons between football and baseball or basketball difficult. A basketball team plays around 86 games, and it seems like a baseball team plays 412. [Laughter.] A football team, though, plays only 10 home games, so the ticket prices naturally will be higher. The squad size is larger in football than in any other sport, and that also raises the cost.

I do want to suggest that an innovation of the National Football League—sharing gate receipts and television revenues equally among the clubs—probably has done more to bring about balance than any reserve system, or the Rozelle Rule, or the waiver system or trading, or anything else.

If the clubs in basketball and the other sports shared revenues more equally, as is done in football—if they moved to a 50-50 split between the home and the visiting club—they would eliminate many problems for fans in places with small stadiums. That would make it easier to achieve more balance.

CONGRESSMAN KEMP: I agree with what Ed Garvey said, but I would like to comment on a point that Roger Noll made earlier. If Congress were to look objectively at professional sports, he said, it would ultimately conclude that a climate of total competition should be established. Then the players would have a totally free market, and, if a franchise failed and threatened the league, that financial disaster would have to be prevented through the political process.

As long as fans can buy a ticket or abstain from buying a ticket, they are protected by the mechanism of the free marketplace. In other words, they have freedom of choice. But as soon as those fans become taxpaying supporters of the sport, they will have to subsidize the Senators to keep the club in Washington, or subsidize some other franchise that is losing money and that might want to move. Those decisions, I believe, should be subject to market forces, which have been praised here in some areas. The market is what makes the difference. As bad as it is to hear a threat of a move by the Yankees, or by the Jets, or to watch the Dodgers move from New York to Los Angeles, such things are better than the alternative of government regulation. I agree with Sam Ervin and with the late Senator Hart, who both looked into this issue in an objective way, without any ideological bias. They concluded that the market was a better influence on the franchise operation than was the political process or bureaucratic process.

PROFESSOR NOLL: That's obviously true. I agree completely.

CONGRESSMAN KEMP: I thought I heard you say that the franchise should be protected from failures.

PROFESSOR NOLL: No, I said that is what's happening. In fact, the current mechanism works so that a club cannot get into the league unless it can guarantee it won't fail.

CONGRESSMAN KEMP: That's not true of most franchises, though.

PROFESSOR NOLL: In regard to the Senators' move to Dallas, I agree that Bob Short should be able to move his business to Dallas. The reason that we care about it in Washington, D.C., is that somebody else with $10 million was willing to run a Washington club, but was not allowed to do it. We care about teams moving because we cannot replace them. People in New York care about the possibility of the Jets moving to New Jersey because they cannot replace them.

CONGRESSMAN KEMP: I am concerned about teams moving, as well. My point is that the business entity in professional sports is not the individual franchise. The real business entity is the league. The league rises and falls with competitive balance, with the financial success, as Ed Garvey mentioned, of every franchise operator in the league. Over the years, the league has prospered to the extent that it has had strong competition. The league shares not only the revenues but also the talent and made the game as attractive as possible on the field.

MR. MACPHAIL: Professor Noll, suppose you had been a member of the American League and had voted to permit a team in Seattle, Washington, when the owners were not properly financed and their facility was not adequate for major league baseball. And suppose that club went into bankruptcy, and the federal bankruptcy court ordered it sold to Milwaukee. Then suppose your league was sued for deserting Seattle. If all that had happened to you, and then you came to a fairly similar situation, don't you think you would be inclined to vote against granting that franchise?

In your book you, yourself, have pointed out that one of the problems encountered in the financial statements of baseball clubs is the heavy interest expense. That is one of the toughest problems of operating improperly financed clubs—carrying a large interest expense. If a club wants to start without proper financing, such that it would have a large interest expense and not be able to break even, is it wrong for the league to reject that club's application for membership?

PROFESSOR NOLL: No, not in the least. In fact, if I were an owner, I perhaps would be even worse than many of the present owners. I wouldn't be a Phil Wrigley, who is in the sport for the good of his home town. I would probably be a profit maximizer to the nth degree, and there is nothing immoral or wrong or silly or stupid about that.

Owners in sports in general are, almost without exception, good businessmen. They have an established record in enterprises other than baseball to prove it, and in financial matters they behave in a sensible way. Obviously, if they want to collect $12 million for an expansion franchise—or going back to the Seattle days, $6 million—they want to make certain that the purchaser can actually pay it. If I were an owner, I would deal out the franchises very slowly, at a very high price, and only to gold-plated enterprises.

But that policy is not necessarily in the best interest of the sport as a whole—it does not incorporate the best interests of the fans, the players, and the owners, all taken together. Rather than selling the franchise in this particular way, an alternative would be to have someone post a bond guaranteeing the complete financial operations of the team for a year and a half. Anyone who wanted to get into the league would have to put $4 million in the Chase Manhattan Bank in a trust which could be used to continue operations only if the team folded.

MR. GARVEY: Or let the players association hold it.

PROFESSOR NOLL: You go to the Riviera too often already, Garvey. [Laughter.]

MR. DALY: We have covered a very broad area but there is something more I would like to ask. Is the consensus among you that self-regulation would be the most desirable course, rather than an increase in government intervention?

CONGRESSMAN KEMP: You'd better ask each participant. [Laughter.]

MR. DALY: The Sisk Committee [House Select Committee on Professional Sports] took particular note of player violence, drug use, working conditions, and safety. Are all of these areas susceptible to a satisfactory resolution within the body politic of the industry itself, without direct government intervention?

MR. GARVEY: In many areas, the industry can address the problems raised by the Sisk Committee. Certainly, football is a violent game, but the players themselves can form committees to control unnecessary violence, and that is probably the most effective way of controlling it. On the question of player agents, our union is working on that problem. We have held some seminars and we are trying to upgrade the professional level of representatives.

On general safety, we, like other industries, have to turn to the Occupational Safety and Health Administration and, unfortunately, the Consumer Product Safety Commission on matters like artificial turf. Some people might call that interference, but the union itself is not strong enough to tell a club to rip up its artificial turf because it is causing injuries and shortening the careers of our players.

We hope the government will do something to aid the union in its effort. Otherwise, without the protection of the federal courts, the National Labor Relations Board, and other government agencies, the union could be in deep trouble in professional sports. The owners tend to have enormous power, as we have seen in all sports. So, we have to rely to a certain extent on the protective arm of government.

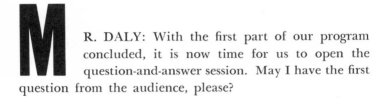

R. DALY: With the first part of our program concluded, it is now time for us to open the question-and-answer session. May I have the first question from the audience, please?

MORT ROSENBERG, attorney, Library of Congress: Mr. Garvey, you discussed player agents, and you mentioned the efforts of the players association to make them honest and fair to the players. But the Sisk Committee report indicated that perhaps there is still a problem in the player–agent field. A recent series of articles in *Newsday* reflects that there may be a scandal in the way player agents deal with players and coaches and those still in the amateur ranks. Could you comment on first whether one players association can be effective, or, must there be a banding together of players associations? Second, if the players associations cannot be effective, will the federal government have to take a hand either in passing federal criminal legislation or in requiring registration or some kind of broker–dealer arrangement?

MR. GARVEY: We have had five seminars for lawyers and agents who represent the professional athlete, and those seminars have also involved the hockey players association and the basketball players association. We are taking steps to work particularly with National Basketball Association players for certification of lawyers and agents, to force them at least to disclose whom they represent, whether they get a power of attorney, and whether they take a percentage or an hourly rate. Then we can distribute information to the college juniors and seniors telling them to contact the players association before signing with anyone. We can prepare a model contract and tell them not to agree to anything less favorable than that.

Beyond that, the Justice Department could do much to help us clean up in the area of white collar crime. I don't know if any specific legislation would help. If the four player unions work together, perhaps, in cooperation with the Justice Department, we can do just about everything we have to.

ROGER SPENCER, economist, Securities and Exchange Commission: Many years ago, baseball was given an exemption from the antitrust laws because it was considered to be a sport rather than a business. There seems to have been no discussion about that differentiation tonight. Does that mean we now consider baseball, football, and other similar activities to be businesses rather than sports? If they were deemed sports rather than businesses, would that reduce the reason for government activity?

CONGRESSMAN KEMP: I think there has been a discussion of that very issue all evening. In my opening statement, I made the point that professional sports should be treated as a business. They are a business, and for the business to succeed, there should be some partial antitrust exemptions to allow limited competitive practices that make the game attractive to fans and successful at the gate. That is why I favor some legislation that would cover all sports and help resolve the exemption that was granted to baseball in the 1920s by the Supreme Court. Professional football, baseball, hockey, and basketball should be allowed to understand the ground rules under which they are operating.

PROFESSOR NOLL: The pedagogue in me must correct the premise of the question. Mr. Justice Holmes did not rule that baseball was a sport and not a business. He ruled that it was not engaged in interstate commerce. In his opinion in the *Federal Baseball League* case, Holmes likened baseball to the old Chautauqua lecture programs. In fact, Holmes said it was a business, but that most people who attend baseball games do not cross state lines to do so. Therefore, the interstate commerce clause of the Constitution granted it immunity from the federal antitrust laws.

MR. GARVEY: It is bad enough when accountants try to practice law, but when economists start doing it—[Laughter.]

The Supreme Court has admitted that this decision is an "aberration" and has almost begged Congress to put all sports on the same level. I am against any kind of exemption from antitrust laws for any practice. In the *Mackey* case, the *Yazoo Smith* case, and the *Kapp* case, we established that federal judges can look at the sport of football as they examine any other industry to determine whether the restrictive practice in question is reasonable or unreasonable under the antitrust laws. There is no need for any legislation except to remove baseball's exemption and to put it on the same plane as the other sports. Then we'll all be happy.

MR. DALY: In this area, the labor exemption is probably germane, Mr. Garvey. Would you discuss how the labor exemption applies to the fundamental issues of antitrust?

27

MR. GARVEY: When the Supreme Court decided that football was different from baseball and was covered by the antitrust laws, the football club owners asked Congress to exempt them but not to worry about the athletes who would be covered by the labor laws. When the owners refused to recognize our union in 1970, we went to the National Labor Relations Board, and the owners said that the NLRB should not take jurisdiction because the players would be protected by other laws.

Ultimately a theory evolved that the federal courts should not hold the owners to a strict antitrust standard in a situation that has an impact on the athletes' working conditions, such as the reserve system, if it is a mandatory subject of collective bargaining. Instead, the parties should be left to work it out themselves. If, as a result of arm's-length collective bargaining, the labor union and the management reach an agreement that restricts player movement, then it should be immune from antitrust attack.

The owners have argued that, as long as a point is a mandatory subject of bargaining, immunity should be granted no matter whether the point was really bargained or not. We in the union have been arguing strenuously that if the restriction in question benefits the workers and the majority of the people in the bargaining unit, then possibly it is exempt from antitrust attack. But we do not claim a blanket immunity. I think this is the law today. This is certainly a major area of controversy in antitrust law and labor law, so we will have to wait and see how it is finally settled.

MR. DALY: The labor exemption applies not only to the sports industry but rather across the whole panorama of the working population in the United States.

MORRIS SIEGEL, sports columnist, *Washington Star:* Mr. Daly, if I may usurp your responsibilities as moderator for a moment, I would like to introduce the head coach of the Baltimore Colts, Ted Marchibroda, and the head of professional scouting for the Redskins, Bobby Mitchell. [Applause.]

I want to direct this question to Lee MacPhail. In his defense of franchise jumping, he asked what the baseball leagues can do when owners are underfinanced. He cited the Seattle team, which the bankruptcy court ordered to be sold. He cited the Washington team—which he made a desperate effort to keep here. The American League and the baseball commissioner later suggested that Bob Short was also underfinanced when he moved the team. Another prime example of underfinancing has also occurred in Cleveland. Yet the American League voted those teams into the league. Why should each of these cities have to suffer for an American League blunder?

MR. MACPHAIL: I agree that those teams were indeed underfinanced, and I would not claim that the decisions of the American League have always been perfect.

Some of those decisions go back some time. Mr. Short already owned the club here when it moved. Often we have been confronted with a club that has to be sold, perhaps because of financial distress, and we had to make the best arrangement we could. Perhaps we knew that the new owners were not financed as well as we would like, but there were no other owners around. Someone has to operate a club.

In Cleveland right now there is no one to operate a National Hockey League team. The players have not been paid and apparently will be free agents.

CONGRESSMAN KEMP: The heart of the matter is that it ought not to be the concern of the United States Congress whether or not a sound economic decision was made. The antitrust

29

laws ought not to be used capriciously. Pro sports clubs should not be bludgeoned into a city or out of a city, or into changing a decision. I agree with Senator Sam Ervin who said that the problems we have would only be exacerbated if they were moved from the market—with all its faults—to Congress.

MR. GARVEY: I don't know anything about markets, but I do remember when the Milwaukee Braves moved, because I grew up near there. The team moved to Atlanta, in my judgment, because it obtained a television contract that would give the team an increase in short-term dollars. The club moved away from a city that deserved baseball and had supported baseball.

If Congress simply will not test the owners against any standard, including antitrust, it is inviting the kind of abuse that was clearly present in that case. It makes sense to remove that exemption and to set up some sort of standard for allowing a team to move. It is a severe blow to a city when it loses a franchise. It would be a strong threat to the city of New York or to the twin cities in Minnesota to lose their teams if a new stadium is not built. Congress should at least look into this problem.

PROFESSOR NOLL: As Congressman Kemp pointed out, relying on the market makes a great deal of sense. But relying on the market means more than merely letting a team move from one city to another because the market is better there. Relying on a market also means letting people go out of business if they face financial difficulties. It also means allowing people into the business when they perceive a market to be there. And all of those features of the market are not present in professional sports today.

Although I hate to sound like a lawyer again, I must point out that by a longstanding principle of antitrust law, the prospect of financial loss is not a legally viable antitrust defense. Obviously, if a monopoly is broken up through antitrust, it faces a financial loss. Expressing fear of such a loss is no argument against the claim that there ought to be competition. Of course, there will be financial loss through competition, but the whole point of the market is a Darwinian survival of the fittest. Those who run a business correctly will survive and prosper. Those who do not will not have a Dallas to run to because Dallas will already have another team.

MR. MACPHAIL: If the leagues lose their control of the movement of franchises—whether through antitrust or government legislation or some other way—that just increases the chances for clubs to move. The Milwaukee move to Atlanta should have been stopped by the National League, but if we take away its power to do that, then there will be no control, no stability, and no permanence.

PROFESSOR NOLL: Why shouldn't the people in Atlanta have a team?

MR. MACPHAIL: I think they should, and they do have one, and so do the people in Milwaukee.

PROFESSOR NOLL: Okay. Fine. [Laughter.]

MICHAEL CANES, professional economist, American Petroleum Institute: I have a question for Mr. Garvey. I can understand why you approve of the recent court decisions reducing restrictions in the players markets. One consequence has been that teams compete for players, as each team seeks to field a winning team and bids up player prices in an effort to do so. The net result for the league, since the number of games played remains exactly the same and the wages for the players are higher, is that the costs to the team owners are greater. Possibly some of these costs are passed on to the fans in higher ticket prices. These wage increases also reduce the financial strength of the franchises, and some may go under as a consequence.

Aren't these results inimical to the interest of the fans? Aren't the fans worse off than they were when we had restrictions in the players market?

MR. GARVEY: On behalf of the fans, I would like to suggest some consequences that flow from the court decisions and the elimination of the restrictions.

First, they have brought about collective bargaining for the first time. The owners in the past, because of their enormous power in comparison with the union, could simply say they would not change that system. When the courts said the owners had to change the system because it was illegal, suddenly they proposed to bargain about the restrictions. That has been the first positive thing from our point of view.

Secondly, we do not believe—and I'm playing the economist here—that ticket prices have anything to do with player salaries. I'm sure that heads will shake over that, but when the Washington Redskins set their ticket price level, they essentially determine what the people will pay to watch the game, instead of staying home or doing something else. The prices will not go up simply because the club signs a free agent like John Riggins or Calvin Hill. It makes that decision independently of their players' salaries at that particular time. Obviously, if costs go up, the fans ultimately bear some of that cost, but we will never know whether any team in the National Football League raised its ticket prices because of increased player costs or increased interest rates or some other factor.

CONGRESSMAN KEMP: At the risk of disagreeing, I will say the cost of production, whether it is the interest on a loan or the cost of labor or some other cost, obviously is a factor in the cost of the ticket. I happen to think that a profit is also a cost of production and should be treated as such. An enterprise has to make a profit to keep going, and it should be considered like other costs.

The agreements negotiated in the last several years will raise costs. It should be obvious that all of these costs are subject to the forces of the market. Without trying to sound too much like an economic theorist, I would repeat that the players and their representatives are subject to the same market processes as everyone else is.

There is a risk of killing the goose, so to speak, that is laying a golden egg. Every union and every business has to sell its product at a price consistent with its ability to meet costs, make a profit, and attract the fans. Its success can be tested only in the marketplace, it seems to me. If the Redskins raise their prices too high, fan interest will ultimately fall off, and the club will be hurt in the worst possible place—the pocketbook. The fans' ultimate protection and/or prerogative is also their greatest power ever over a business— the right to buy or to abstain from buying a particular product. That right should be protected as much as possible.

MR. MACPHAIL: I agree with Congressman Kemp on that. Athletes' salaries these days are very alarming because it is hard to see how professional sports can continue with this added expense.

A few years ago, the owners had too much advantage in negotiating contracts with players, but the pendulum has swung the other way. In this new situation, clubs are offering everything they have to the new free agents. I think the pendulum will swing back—it will have to. It is the marketplace that will determine this. There will be a little more restraint, a little more economic reasonableness on the part of the clubs, and players' salaries will return to a more logical level.

PROFESSOR NOLL: If Mike Canes is correct about teams going under, some teams must now be on the margin so that, if their costs go up a little, that will be the end of the ball game for them. But consider those two outstanding examples of league balance, Seattle and Tampa in the National Football League. Those teams came into the league with very bad players, as is normal in an expansion. The owners were willing to pay $16 million for the right to operate a team in the league, given the antitrust and union environment at the time. One might anticipate that the competition in the player market, which drove wages up, would thereby drive down the value of that $16 million enterprise. But those teams now command a positive price—that is to say, they return enough profit so that somebody is willing to pay more than zero to acquire them. And neither club has a factory attached to it, or much of anything else except some equipment and a few desks. There is little capital investment in the physical assets of a team. The investment is basically in the right to belong to a league.

Such rights have value primarily because of various restrictive practices, like those in the player market. If we take away some of those restrictive practices, the value of league membership will fall. But in order for the teams to stop operating, the value would have to fall below zero—that is to say, the team would have to start losing so much money that no one would be willing to buy it.

I find it unlikely that the Tampa Bay Buccaneers will fall in value from $16 million to $0 because of an agreement signed with the players association or because of the loss of an antitrust case with regard to players, or that baseball franchises will fall from $12 million to $0 because of what happened with their players association. The clubs may suffer a relative financial loss, but there is little threat that many of them will go under.

CONGRESSMAN KEMP: I'm trying to figure out what I heard.

MR. GARVEY: You heard that if Ted Marchibroda coached in Tampa Bay, they would win. [Laughter.]

CONGRESSMAN KEMP: I agree, although coach McKay is a great one, too, that's part of what makes pro football such a great game. Professor Noll spoke about expansion franchises. The Miami Dolphins, a few years ago, were an expansion franchise in the American Football League, and the team was marginal for many years, but it ended up winning the Super Bowl. Such things can happen, and some of the practices that Professor Noll decries have helped make them happen. These practices can be modified or negotiated, and they should be. Nonetheless, those practices allowed me and many other professional athletes to earn good incomes and to enhance our own after-sport career possibilities.

American sports today are an entertainment business and subject to the same fickleness from the public as other entertainment. There is no guarantee that a franchise worth $12 million today will be worth $12 million tomorrow. The entertainment industry as a whole changes and fluctuates, and it is very capricious and risky.

To stake future negotiations on the gross value of a franchise operation disregards the fact that it is a volatile business. There is no guarantee that any sport will always rank high in popularity. Each club has to be careful to remain in harmony with its public and to maintain a working link between the employees and the employer. The relationship should be a partnership, not class warfare. Before any steps are taken, their effect on the climate and profitability of the business should be considered.

The profit incentive is no different from the wage incentive. Both are honorable, both should be pursued, and over the years both have been pursued to the benefit of everybody, including the fans, especially in the National Football League and in professional baseball. But the fans must be represented too, and they make their voices heard in more ways than one.

Tom Seppy, Associated Press: Congressman Kemp, don't you believe that fans who pay taxes for the building of new stadiums should be protected in some way in the annual bidding to move teams from one city to another? Before the House sports committee last fall, the counsel for the city of Buffalo was very concerned over an attempt to move a team from Buffalo to Florida. Shouldn't the federal government try to protect a city from attempts to take away its team after the taxpayers have indebted themselves over many, many years to build a facility?

Congressman Kemp: I know a little bit about that situation in Buffalo. There was a debate over whether that stadium should be built as a municipal stadium or as a privately financed stadium. I take some pride that I was one who said the taxpayers ought not to build it, that it ought to be built privately. It could have been done privately, I am convinced. Of course, that is academic at this point because the county ended up financing a new 80,000-seat stadium to keep the Buffalo Bills.

A municipality or county that allows a franchise to become such an intimidating factor should be held accountable in the election process. That accountability could be settled far better in Buffalo or Erie County, where the people are close to the situation, than in Washington, D.C., where the government is not necessarily as omnipotent or omniscient as many people would have us believe. The

Buffalo situation worked out far better than it would have if Congress had held hearings in Buffalo and undertaken to bludgeon the Buffalo Bills through antitrust or other legislation.

On this issue, I was on the side of both the fans and the taxpayers, because I just don't think it should have been a municipally built stadium in the first place.

MR. DALY: Do you believe that should be true nationally?

CONGRESSMAN KEMP: That is the premise upon which my answer is based—yes, sir. Obviously we are speaking hypothetically and I am talking about the ideal situation rather than the real one. But taxpayers carry the burden and, wherever possible, we must lighten that burden.

MR. GARVEY: Put yourself in the position of a mayor or councilman in a city that is about to lose its franchise unless he gives the club a stadium for a dollar for the first million fans and grants other concessions. Local officials are in a terrible bind when a club can threaten to move to Phoenix or New York unless the city builds a new stadium. There may be many statesmen out there who are capable of handling that kind of pressure, but I would guess the only way to handle it effectively is for the Congress to set up some sort of regulation.

PROFESSOR NOLL: Congressman Kemp is right as a matter of theory, but he tends to be impractical, unlike us academics. [Laughter.]

He does not realize that there are about twenty-five stadiums for baseball and football, and about an equal number for basketball, already built and owned publicly. Even if we could somehow wave a magic wand and make certain that all stadiums built in the future would be private, there would still be a problem.

The answer to the question is that there is a problem because of a scarcity of teams. If somebody is willing to go into the business of basketball in Florida again, after observing the failures in the past, why shouldn't a team be formed? For every fan in Buffalo who got off the hook because the team did not leave, there is a fan in Florida who did not get a team. It is a zero-sum game—if somebody wins, somebody else loses. The problem is that there is one team, and two cities want it. There is no mechanism in the existing structure of sports to make sure that there are two teams when two cities each want one.

CONGRESSMAN KEMP: Do you think cities have some right, some constitutional protection, to buy into a football or baseball league?

PROFESSOR NOLL: No, they don't need a constitutional amendment.

CONGRESSMAN KEMP: Should anyone be able to buy a McDonald's franchise? There is no guarantee that anyone can own a franchise, but anyone can start a football league or a baseball league or a fast-food chain, as difficult and impractical as that sounds. I started in a new league—the American Football League. Others include the World Football League, the Canadian League, and the All America Conference.

Let's look back at some of the failures of professional sports franchises and leagues. Incidentally, I would grant Ed Garvey's point that the World Football League had far greater problems than I am addressing here because the league did lack competitive balance to attract the fans and an institutional framework—which Professor Noll has said is not needed. Some in the AFL were uncompetitive—and could not keep up in the player market. Denver almost failed in 1965 or 1966 because it could not keep up with the National Football League in the bidding war. There were several other teams in the American Football League that also were having trouble. My point is, yes, we can let teams fail, but, if we had, we would not have twenty-eight football teams today in professional football, and we would not have 1,600 jobs. Those are important considerations.

PROFESSOR NOLL: We would have more teams and more jobs with more competition. In order to use the formation of a league as the mechanism for promoting competition, there must be at least eight or ten cities that can support a new team. If there are just two or four or six cities that do not have a team but could support one, they must await expansion, for their numbers are insufficient to form a league. As long as an existing league keeps the number of cities in this category low enough so that a new league is not likely to succeed, it can retain a monopoly.

What happened with the World Football League is an interesting phenomenon. At the time the league was folding, the number of teams in it changed from day to day. About two-thirds of the cities in the league simply were not supporting their teams. But four teams were breaking even, or very nearly so, and two of them wanted to join the National Football League. So some cities in that WFL were viable, but there were not enough to maintain the new league. How long should those cities have to wait to be admitted to the NFL? Should they have to wait two or three more decades until there are ten cities that can support teams, and then form a league to compete with the National Football League for three or four years before merging with it to reestablish the monopoly? Do we have to do it that way?

CONGRESSMAN KEMP: No, we don't. But there were twelve teams just a decade and a half ago, and there are twenty-eight today. In practice, things have worked out far better than your theoretical model would suggest.

JACK PEARCE, lawyer, Pearce and Brand: Congressman Kemp, we all agree that sports are a business. Some observers take the position that a kind of laissez-faire should prevail with immunities from the antitrust laws. These laws generally promote competition and ease of entry. Isn't that position tantamount to letting sports operate as a business but with an opportunity to make a greater than competitive profit for the owners and the players?

My second question is addressed to Mr. Garvey. If the owners were required to adhere to the ordinary antitrust standards in all respects, should not the players also?

CONGRESSMAN KEMP: My position is that laissez-faire should not prevail in sports, that they should be treated as a business, that they should come under antitrust, and that baseball should not be exempt from antitrust.

Ed Garvey and I have had a disagreement for a long time—an honest one, a sincere one. It is simply this: I believe there should be a limited antitrust exemption for practices that make the game attractive to the fan who ultimately must pay for wages, fringe benefits, and, indeed, profits.

I do not know what those profits are. There are other businesses whose profits I do not know. It is not necessarily my job in the Congress of the United States to determine those profits. As a player, however, I accepted certain limited restrictions on my freedom to trade my services in the marketplace. I understood that those restrictions were in my interest because they allowed the game to be profitable enough to employ me and O. J. Simpson and hundreds of other players at a rate for which we were willing to play. All of us probably thought or think we were underpaid.

I hope that gets at your question. I am not for a free market in sports franchises, and I think they should come under antitrust. In a short period of time, the present practices of the National Football League have brought about vast increases in the amount of football being played and in the number of people watching it. And the pricing must be relatively effective because the fans keep buying tickets. Moreover, those practices have done much to advance the cause of the players.

Frankly, I do not think Congress should get into that business or do to professional sports what has been done to the postal delivery service, the railroads, the supply of natural gas, and other areas of American life today.

MR. GARVEY: I guess I could say that Congressman Kemp and I have a few minor differences. We at the players association are just trying to do for the players what Congress has recently done for Congress, in terms of wages. If we can do what Congress has done, we will be all right. [Laughter.]

It is too simple to say now that government should not become involved. It has already waded in and given the owners vast power and exacted nothing in return. And now some people want to let the union take the burden.

There are about twenty-eight locals within the National Football League, made up of, say, forty-five members each. In terms of salary level, the players can anticipate a career with a lot of competition for a few high-paying jobs. To ask this entity to take on the government-aided monopoly would amount to abandoning the whole battle.

Certainly, if it were not for the courts and the National Labor Relations Board, we would be nowhere, because we just do not have sufficient strength. Should we be subject to antitrust laws? Of course not. No labor union should be. It has been the policy of this country for a long time that unions will not be. All we want is a guaranteed wage, and then we'll let them worry about whether or not the business fails. We'll be all right. [Laughter.]

MR. DALY: This concludes another public policy forum. On behalf of the American Enterprise Institute, our heartfelt thanks to the distinguished panelists, Congressman Kemp, Mr. Garvey, Professor Noll, and Mr. MacPhail, and to our guests in the audience for their participation.